MW00511274

Hydroponics for beginners

The Ultimate Beginner's Guide To Quickly Start To Grow Fruits, Herbs And Vegetables Hydroponically At Home.

A Precise Guide On Home Techniques, Aquaponics And Hydroponics.

|2021 Edition|

© Copyright 2021 by William Brown

TABLE OF CONTENTS

Legal & Disclaimer

The information contained in this book and its contents is not designed to replace or take the place of any form of medical or professional advice; and is not meant to replace the need for independent medical, financial, legal or other professional advice or services, as may be required. The content and information in this book have been provided for educational and entertainment purposes only.

The content and information contained in this book has been compiled from sources deemed reliable, and it is accurate to the best of the Author's knowledge, information and belief. However, the Author cannot guarantee its accuracy and validity and cannot be held liable for any errors and/or omissions. Further, changes are periodically made to this book as and when needed. Where appropriate and/or necessary, you must consult a professional (including but not limited to your doctor, attorney, financial advisor or such other professional advisor) before using any of the suggested remedies, techniques, or information in this book.

Upon using the contents and information contained in this book, you agree to hold harmless the Author from and against any damages, costs, and expenses, including any legal fees potentially resulting from the application of any of the information provided by this book. This disclaimer applies to any loss, damages or injury caused by the use and application, whether directly or indirectly, of any advice or information presented, whether for breach of contract, tort, negligence, personal injury, criminal intent, or under any other cause of action.

You agree to accept all risks of using the information presented inside this book.

You agree that by continuing to read this book, where appropriate and/or necessary, you shall consult a professional (including but not limited to your doctor, attorney, or financial advisor or such other advisor as needed) before using any of the suggested remedies, techniques, or information in this book.

INTRODUCTION

Hydroponics is a technique of growing plants in nutrient solutions with or without the use of an inert medium such as gravel, vermiculite, rockwool, peat moss, saw dust, coir dust, coconut fibre, etc. to provide mechanical support. The term Hydroponics was derived from the Greek words: *hydro - means water and ponos* - means labour and literally means water work. The word hydroponics was coined by Professor William Gericke in the early 1930s; describe the growing of plants with their roots suspended in water containing mineral nutrients. Researchers at Purdue University developed the nutriculture system in 1940. During 1960s and 70s, commercial hydroponics farms were developed in Arizona, Abu Dhabi, Belgium, California, Denmark, German, Holland, Iran, Italy, Japan, Russian Federation and other countries. Most hydroponic systems operate automatically to control the amount of water, nutrients and photoperiod based on the requirements of different plants (Resh, 2013). Due to rapid urbanization and industrialization not only, the cultivable land is decreasing but also conventional agricultural practices causing a wide range of negative impacts on the environment. To sustainably feed the world's growing population, methods for growing sufficient food have to evolve. Modification in growth medium is an alternative for sustainable production and to conserve fast depleting land and available water resources. In the present scenario, soil less cultivation might be commenced successfully and considered as alternative option for growing healthy food plants, crops or vegetables (Butler and Oebker, 2006). Agriculture without soil includes hydro agriculture (Hydroponics), aqua agriculture (Aquaponics) and aerobic agriculture (Aeroponics) as well as substrate culture. Among these hydroponics techniques is gaining popularity because of its efficient management of resources and food production. Various commercial and specialty crops can be grown using hydroponics including leafy vegetables, tomatoes, cucumbers, peppers, strawberries, and many more.

THE SCIENCE BEHIND HYDROPONICS

IS HYDROPONICS A SCIENCE?

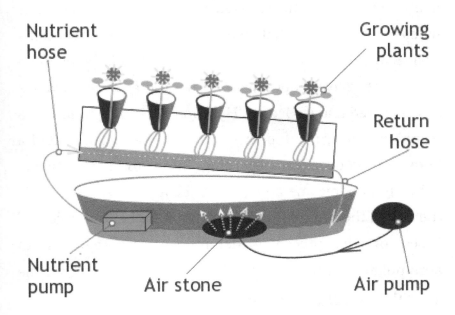

This question has been frequently asked without a definite answer. Most dictionaries do not define hydroponics as a science, but rather as another means of growing or cultivating plants. However, the

Webster's New World College Dictionary, fourth edition (1999), does define hydroponics as "the science of growing or the production of plants in a nutrient-rich solution." Not even in the Wikipedia (www.wikipedia.com)definition and accompanying description of hydroponics does the word "science" appear. Probably the only organization actively engaged in the science aspect is the National Aeronautic Space Administration (NASA)since some form of hydroponics will be the selected method for grow-ing plants in space or on celestial bodies. The Merriam Webster's Collegiate Dictionary's definition for science is "something (as a sport or technique) that may be studied or learned like systematized knowledge. "Hydroponics is indeed a technique for growing plants and there has accumulated a body of knowledge regarding how to grow plants using hydroponic method (or should it be the hydroponic method?), therefore fitting the criterion for being a "science" based on the preceding definition. Also, there is an accumulated body of "systemized knowledge" that fits the second part of the science definition.

Science has always been around us, as has water. Hydroponic growing is a united entity of both. Having the endless amounts of liquids wash the gentle roots of your plants will improve its overall health. This is not the only use of hydroponics in gardening, though. Here are some of the most interesting and important facts that science has in support of changing your soil into a hydroponic system.

There is a rule which makes growing hydroponically the top choice for many professionals. Hydroponics is an impeccable partner for growing any type of plants, but what makes it the perfect companion for any farmer? This is the fact that hydroponics depends on a special type of water, cleansed, which does not include any chemicals of its own (or if it does, they are not enough to influence the plants).

This is why you can make any hydroponic system ideal by adding the needed hydroponic nutrients. Because of the scientific discoveries in the field, many companies have already found out what are the most advanced nutrients for growing hydroponically and getting huge yields in the same time.

One of the most important scientific positives of hydroponics is that the water in the system can be reused. Unlike soil, the liquids can be easily maintained and just by cleansing or adding more nutrients or supplements, one can reuse the same medium.

This makes hydroponics much cheaper and easier to maintain. Scientifically explained, this is because water does not connect directly to the nutrients as would soil and instead just makes them circulate around the root mass, leaving everything available for the plant itself.

Thirdly, getting rid of pests and diseases has never been easier. By growing hydroponically, you will find out that all you need is to cleanse the liquids off the inflection. It's very easy as everything is found in a single (okay, for the bigger farms it might be more than one) container which is very mobile.

The only issue is the fact that you will have to refill the system with new nutrients and supplements, but this should not be a problem as hydroponic nutrients usually take care of everything, if used properly.

Last but not least, with no need for soil in hydroponic growing the process itself becomes much cleaner and tidier. Yes, this is not science, but cleaning it would have been as hard as dividing atoms at home.

Naturally, there are issues in hydroponic growing as well. After all, it should have some negative sides, right? The biggest problem is that once you get your plants sick, which is not that easy, the infection would spread very fast and is an almost certain death of all plants that are connected to the same system.

This said, the illness usually comes from some of the plants themselves as the nutrients or water can hardly bring anything harmful alone. Hence, if you take care of the machines and systems, if you take seeds and seedlings from a trusted supplier, everything will be perfectly fine.

TYPES OF HYDROPONICS SYSTEMS

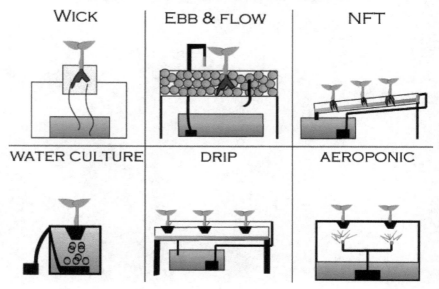

Hydroponics is a way of cultivating plants, by providing nutrients they need to grow in water. Although no soil is used, a medium may be used for the roots to soak and provide constant water supply. Such mediums lead us to think about hydroponics systems, which are discussed below.

Basically, there are 6 types of hydroponics systems, including wick, water culture, ebb & flow (also known as flood & drain), drip, nutrient film technique (NFT), and aeroponic. Although there are many variations on these 6 systems, all hydroponics methods are a combination these 6.

THE WICK SYSTEM

This is simplest hydroponic system requiring no electricity, pump and aerators (Shrestha and Dunn, 2013). Plants are placed in an absorbent medium like coco coir, vermiculite, perlite with a nylon wick running from plant roots into a reservoir of nutrient solution. Water or nutrient solution supplied to plants through capillary action. This system works well for small plants, herbs and spice and doesn't work effectively that needs lot of water

By far the simplest type of system, the wick system is a passive hydroponics system, meaning that there are no moving parts in it. The nutrient solution is gets drawn into the growing medium from a reservoir with a wick. The wick system is able to use several plant growing mediums such as Perlite, Vermiculite, Pro-Mix, and Coconut Fiber- all of these being the most popular.

There is a disadvantage associated with the wick system, which is that the plants are large or the nutrient solution may use up a lot of water, much quicker than the wick system can supply it.

WATER CULTURE

Deepwater Culture (DWC), also known as the reservoir method, is by far the easiest method for growing plants with hydroponics. In a Deepwater Culture hydroponic system, the roots are suspended in a nutrient solution. An aquarium air pump oxygenates the nutrient solution, this keeps the roots of the plants from drowning. Remember to prevent light from penetrating your system, as this can cause algae to grow. This will wreak havoc on your system.

The primary benefit to using a Deepwater Culture system is that there are no drip or spray emitters to clog. This makes DWC an excellent choice for organic hydroponics, as hydroponics systems that use organic nutrients are more prone to clogs

Of all active hydroponics systems, the water culture is the simplest one. A Styrofoam system is the platform that holds the plant and floats directly on the nutrient solution. Air is supplied to the air stone by an air pump, and bubbles are thus caused to the nutrient solution, providing oxygen to the roots of the plant.

The water culture hydroponics system is ideal for cultivating leaf lettuce, given the fact that these grow rather fast through this system. However, few other plans grow well with the water culture hydroponics system.

Additionally, the water culture hydroponics system is very popular with teachers, for a very inexpensive system can be made out of an old aquarium or water tight containers.

The biggest disadvantage of the water culture hydroponics system is that it does not suit large or long-term plants.

EBB & FLOW SYSTEM

An ebb & flow hydroponics system, also known as a flood and drain system, is a great system for growing plants with hydroponics. This type of system functions by flooding the growing area with the nutrient solution at specific intervals. The nutrient solution then slowly drains back into the reservoir. The pump is hooked to a timer, so the process repeats itself at specific intervals so that your plants get the desired amount of nutrients.

An ebb & flow hydroponics system is ideal for plants that are accustomed to periods of dryness. Certain plants flourish when they go through a slight dry period because it causes the root system to grow larger in search of moisture. As the root system grows larger the plant grows faster because it can absorb more nutrients.

The Ebb and Flow hydroponics system temporarily floods the plant grow tray with nutrient solution and then drains the solution back into the reservoir. A submerged pump is usually connected to a timer in this system. The timer pumps the nutrient solution onto the grow tray. The nutrient solution flows back into the reservoir when the time is turned off. It is set to be activated several times a day, depending on the size and type of plant, temperature, humidity and the kind of plant growing medium that is used.

The Ebb & Flow hydroponics system can be used with several plant growing mediums. The grow tray can be filled with gravel or granular Rockwool, or grow rocks. If individual pots are filled with the plant growing medium, it is easier to move the plants around or even in and out of the system.

The disadvantage associated with the Ebb & Flow system is that some plant growing mediums such as grow rocks and gravel may be susceptible to power outages as well as pump and time failures. Consequently, the plant roots can dry out quickly when the watering cycles are interrupted. This issue can be addressed somewhat though through using growing media that store more water, such as can be relieved somewhat by using growing media that retains more water, such as Rockwool, vermiculite and coconut fiber.

DRIP SYSTEMS - RECOVERY / NON-RECOVERY

A hydroponic drip system is rather simple. A drip system works by providing a slow feed of nutrient solution to the hydroponics medium. We recommend using a slow draining medium, such as Rockwool, coconut coir, or peat moss. You can also use a faster draining medium, although you will have to use a faster dripping emitter.

The downside to a system like this is that the drippers / emitter are famous for clogging. We prefer not to use drip systems, but it can be an effective method for growing if you can avoid the clogs that plague this type of system. The reason the system gets clogged is because particles from nutrients that build up in the emitter. Systems that use organic nutrients are more likely to have this kind of issue.

The most widely used type of hydroponics systems in the world are the drip systems. They are easier to operate, and a timer controls a submerged pump. When the timer activates the pump, the nutrient solution drips onto the base of each plant by a small drip line.

There are two types of drip systems, Recovery Drip and Non-Recovery Drip System. In the Recovery Drip system, the left-over nutrient solution is accumulated back into the reservoir for re-use, whereas in the Non-Recover Drip system, the excess nutrient solution is not collected back into the reservoir. In the recovery drip system, therefore, the timer is inexpensive and efficient since it does not require an accurate control of the watering cycle. On the other hand, the non-recovery drip system requires a precise timer in order that the watering cycles can be adjusted for the plants to get a sufficient amount of nutrient solution and there is less wastage of the solution. This also means, then, that less maintenance is required of the non-recovery system, whereas the recovery system can have large shifts in the nutrient strength levels routinely need checking and adjusting.

NUTRIENT FILM TECHNIQUE (N.F.T)

Nutrient Film Technique, or NFT, is a type of hydroponic system where a continuous flow of nutrient solution runs over the plants roots. This type of solution is on a slight tilt so that the nutrient solution will flow with the force of gravity.

This type of system works very well because the roots of a plant absorb more oxygen from the air than from the nutrient solution itself. Since only the tips of the roots come in contact with the nutrient solution, the plant is able to get more oxygen which facilitates a faster rate of growth.

The most known of hydroponics systems is the Nutrient Film Technique (N.F.T) system. N.F.T. systems entail a continual supply of nutrient solution and the submersible pump requires no timer. The nutrient solution pumped into the growing tray, flows over the roots of the plants, and then collects back into the reservoir.

In the Nutrient Film Technique, there is generally no growing medium needed other than air. This proves to be an inexpensive system, therefore, since there is no need of replacing the growing medium. The plant is usually supported in a small plastic basket, and the roots dangle into the nutrient solution. The N.F.T hydroponics systems is rather vulnerable to power outages and pump failures, and interruption to the flow of the nutrient solution causes the roots to dry out.

AEROPONIC

Perhaps the most technical of hydroponics systems, the aeroponics systems mainly uses air to function. The roots hang in the air and receive moisture from the nutrient solution. The moistening occurs every few minutes, but because the roots hang in the air (like in the N.F.T. system), they dry out if the moistening cycles are disrupted. In the Aeroponic hydroponics systems, the controlling timer runs the pump for a few seconds every couple of minutes.

Aeroponics is a hydroponics method by which the roots are misted with a nutrient solution while suspended in the air. There are two primary methods to get the solution to the exposed roots. The first method involves a fine spray nozzle to mist the roots. The second method uses what's called a pond fogger. If you decide to use a pond fogger then make sure you use a Teflon coated disc, as this will reduce the amount of maintenance required.

You may have heard of the Aero Garden, which is a commercialized aeroponics system. The Aero Garden is an excellent entry point to aeroponics. It's a turn-key system that requires little setup. It also comes with great support and supplies to get you started.

SYSTEMS

Plants most generally have to be stared in a small amount of medium before they can be placed in the growing area. Seeds are started with no nutrients in the water. Seeds have their own food and don't require any additional nutrients until the first set of leaves appear. Nutrient is added at half strength to encourage root development until it's transplanted. Then full-strength nutrients are used for the rest of the plant's growth. There are two kinds of formulas for plants. One promotes the vegetative growth and the other promotes

Fruiting. A system that has both types of plants will have to have one or the other formulas depending on which crop is more important. There are two methods of growing systems, horizontal and vertical. The following are systems:

1. Bag culture; used commercially in run to waste systems. The hobbyist can also use this inexpensive method in a recirculating system. Bags are filled with a lightweight medium and nutrient is fed to each bag by inexpensive spaghetti tubes. Has the advantage of being able to space the plants as they mature.

- Tomatoes in bag culture.

2. Gutter/NFT; A lot of hobbyists have tried just about everything with this type system.

- Manufactured channels; Square corners help to prevent damming.
- Rain gutter; Metal gutter can oxidize and add undesirable materials to the nutrient solution. Line with plastic sheet. Plastic gutters require total support to keep it strait.
- PVC pipe; most hobbyists use PVC pipes with holes drilled for plants. This system is usually more expensive then bag culture. Too often the roots clog

up the waterways and dam the water causing root rot. Aeration in the root zone may become a problem.

3. Beds; are extra wide channels. Beds can be filled with a growing medium or pots can be placed in the bed so that they will pick up the water from the bed through a wicking action. Pots are the most versatile. Plants can be spaced to meet the plant's needs. I use this method for houseplants and for starting seeds. A 1/4 inch of water can be maintained in beds with pots. Water must be drained well in filled beds. Beds can be made from any material that will hold the weight of the plants and the medium. A plastic film can be used to line construction. Nutrient solution is usually aerated and returned to the bed.

Although there is no soil in a hydroponic garden, the plants must still be anchored. There is a wide range of inert materials which can be used to support plant roots and we call them "growing mediums". Heydite, clay pellets, Perlite, vermiculite, and Rockwool are the most popular media. The hydroponic media that work best are pH neutral, provide ample support for plants, retain moisture, and allow space for good air exchange. The type of media you choose will depend on the size and type of plants you wish to grow, and the type of hydroponic system being used.

For continuous drip systems, course media such as Heydite (a porous shale) or Hydrocorn (clay pellets) are best. The 1/4 " to3/4 " pebbles provide enough free drainage and air space to take advantage of continuous feeding. These media also provide good anchorage for larger plants, and are easy to clean and re-use indefinitely.

Rockwool is also another popular medium. Made from rock which has been melted and spun into fibrous cubes and growing slabs with the texture of insulation, Rockwool provides roots with a good balance of water/oxygen. Small cubes are used for starting seeds and cuttings, 3" or 4" cubes for small plants or intermediate growth, and slabs for larger plants. Rockwool can be used with continuous drip or flood and drain systems. Although it is possible to sterilize and re-use Rockwool, most often it is used only once.

Perlite, made from volcanic rock, is a white, light weight material often used as a soil additive. The 1/8" to 1/4" pellets can be used alone as growing medium, but don't provide enough anchorage for large plants. Perlite is often used to start seed and cuttings, which can easily transplanted after rooting. Vermiculite is use the same way as Perlite, and the two are sometimes mixed together. It is made from heat expanded mica and has a flaky, shiny appearance. Soilless mix such as Pro-mix BX, and Pro-mix lite has the appearance and texture of light soil. Mainly peatmoss, mixed with Perlite, it contains very little nutrient, and is used a soil additive, or alone as a hydroponic medium.

Some hydroponic systems do not require any growing medium at all. Various methods are used to support the plants while the roots are directly fed nutrient solution. Some examples of these are, aeroponic, N.F.T., or "Nutrient Film Technique" and deep-water culture.

WATERING METHODS

All the plants need are supplied by water. The roots are placed in an inert growing medium. Water, enriched with all the nutrients the plants need, is supplied to the roots by several different methods.

1. Aeroponics; the roots are sprayed with the nutrient solution. This method ensures that the roots get plenty of oxygen to the root system. It has not been proven that this method helps to make plants grow any faster then in other methods. It has some inherent problems such as nozzles getting plugged up. One of the more expensive methods of hydroponics.

2. Ebb and flow; also called flood and drain. Periodically floods the medium. As the water drains out new air comes in.

Not as hard to maintain as an aeroponics system. Roots can plug up waterways however.

3. NFT; the Nutrient Film Technique is one of the methods most often used by commercial growers. Plant roots are contained in a channel through which a thin "film" of nutrient solution passes. The nutrient solution is aerated and recycled with the addition of makeup water.

4. Run to waste; in this method the nutrient is fed to the plants at near the same rate as the plants use the water. In all the other methods, the nutrient solution returns to a tank to be recycled. This system is the cheapest to get started, however, it requires a lot of monitoring to insure the plants are getting enough nutrient but at the same time not getting too much nutrient. Plants will only take up the nutrients it needs. On sunny days they take up mostly water and leave the nutrients behind to build up. The built-up salts must be purged from the system one or two times a week. This system wastes the most nutrients.

Types of Hydroponics

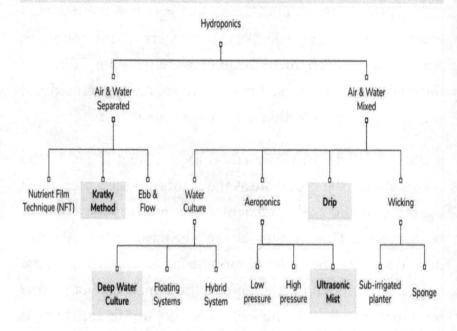

THE COUNTLESS BENEFITS OF HYDROPONIC GARDENING

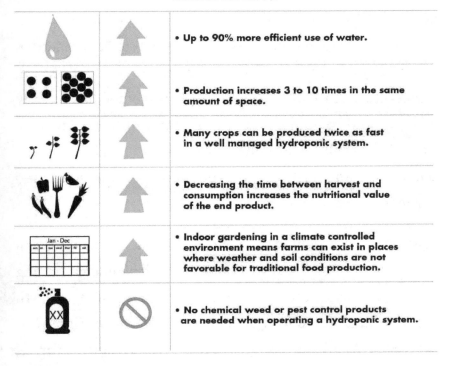

	↑	• Up to 90% more efficient use of water.
	↑	• Production increases 3 to 10 times in the same amount of space.
	↑	• Many crops can be produced twice as fast in a well managed hydroponic system.
	↑	• Decreasing the time between harvest and consumption increases the nutritional value of the end product.
Jan - Dec	↑	• Indoor gardening in a climate controlled environment means farms can exist in places where weather and soil conditions are not favorable for traditional food production.
XX	🚫	• No chemical weed or pest control products are needed when operating a hydroponic system.

Many people are talking about the benefits of hydroponic gardening systems. However, as of yet, these powerful alternatives to more traditional gardening have not fully caught on, but it's definitely gaining ground. As more and more people are seeking ways to grow their own fruits and vegetables, this method is capturing quite a bit of attention. This environmentally friendly, space saving method of gardening is definitely something to be looked into if you're considering growing your own foods.

The benefits of whole food are well known. For many, gardening is a way of getting past rising food costs, and being better able to enjoy healthier foods- right from their gardens. Utilizing hydroponic supplies enables them to have a garden in virtually any space available without worry about season, temperature or weather conditions. This method has actually been around for quite some time, but with a recent push towards urban gardening, has been gaining steady popularity amongst both hobby and production-based gardeners.

Hydroponic gardening is basically, being able to have a garden without using soil. Utilizing a hydroponic gardening system, the plants that you intend to grow are put in a growth medium that allows for nutrients to be delivered directly to the roots. As plants do not actually require soil to thrive, many people find that soil is inefficient. The energy that is used in growing out healthy root systems in soil to find the water and nutrients could be better used in other ways. If readily available nutrition is there for those plants, they often grow up to 50% faster and more healthy.

In utilizing hydroponic supplies, gardeners can gain better control over the nutrient balance in their plants. They can also have better spacing efficiency, utilizing a smaller root system, and reduce water waste with concentrated feeding.

The pH of plants, as well as the nutrient levels are easier to maintain and measure. Having greater control over the gardening conditions can help gardeners not only increase the yield of produce, but also, ensure that crops are at their nutritional peak.

Hydroponic gardening systems are also growing in popularity due to the potential benefits, both societal and environmental. Many have suggested that in using hydroponic supplies, a gardener can create more readily available food to those who may suffer impoverished conditions. Hydroponic gardening systems also ease strains on the environment- with hydroponic supplies that can be set up as recycling both nutrients and water, this reduces needed resources in food production. In these systems, they use as little as 10% of the water that soil-based agriculture needs. It also eliminates the need for pesticide and herbacide use, and fertilizer use is reduced to about 25% of what soil based gardens need.

Hydroponic gardening systems can produce roughly the same amount of food as soil gardens, using 1/5 the space, and are not dependent on growing seasons in many cases. Artificially lit hydroponic gardens can yield year round production, an advantage over traditional gardening methods. Many urban areas already utilize hydroponic gardening systems, as seen in rooftop and basement gardens.

Hydroponics is the act of growing food indoors with the use of lighting equipment and water source that mimics the best of environments in which to grow plants.

Many gardeners are discovering Hydroponics as a valid way to create the food that consume on a daily basis as there are many benefits to hydroponics:

Hydroponics allowed gardening to be done all year round. This means that even in climates which have very short growing seasons, plants, food and flowers can still be cultivated. Hydroponics is an essential development as it removes the limitations that come with climate zones which can be hazardous to growing.

Hydroponics allows for more plants to be grown per given area than traditional gardening. Did you know that Hydroponics factories are able to grow up to ten times as much greenery than traditional gardens? With these areas situated just for growing, they become more effective.

Did you know that with the use of Hydroponics that pests can be practically eliminated? Since the environment in which these plants are grown is indoors - the pests that are found in the natural environment are not able to thrive in the indoors.

Another benefit of Hydroponics is the fact there is no digging or weeding required. There are no plant pieces within the air, and no pesticides are used within the environment because of the lack of pests.

There are many Hydroponic farms that provide food that we eat on a daily basis. Some say that is the future of our food source, as food is grown twice as quickly than it would be in a traditional garden or outdoor environment.

Did you know that Hydroponics has the ability to increase the flavor of the crops? Think about the vegetables that we ingest on a daily basis, the more green the vegetables, the more intense the flavor. There are some aspects of the environment which can take away from the taste of these vegetables. When hydroponics is used, we experience greater taste potential within the vegetables and fruit - as they are in their purest form.

Hydroponic growing allows the gardeners to determine the amount of water that is going to be used on a regular basis. This tight schedule means that all water is going to reach the plants, and less will be wasted. Less wasted water is better for the environment and creates sustainable growing condition.

For anyone interested in growing their own healthy produce but have been put off the idea because of all the hard work involved in running a successful garden, this is for you. I came across this fascinating subject which allows anyone to grow the most amazing plants indoors using hydroponic gardening.

You no longer need to dig in the soil, plant the seeds, water them, weed them and generally spend hour upon hour looking after your plants. Hydroponic gardening allows you to do all this by an ingenious method of allowing he seeds to germinate and grow in special hydroponic systems that use water instead of soil to hold and nourish the plants.

All plants need a plentiful supply of nutrients to sustain a healthy growing cycle and hydroponic gardening does this by adding nutrients directly to the water. This means that the plant roots no longer need to grow far and wide in search of these nutrients and so hydroponic plants do not need the same amount of room to grow in as the plants grown outside in an ordinary garden might need.

You may say that's okay, but what about sunlight, most plants need plenty of sun to grow and thrive. That's very true but in hydroponic gardening the needed sunlight is provided by special bulbs that usually come on and off by setting a timer. Some of the more expensive hydroponic systems provide the gardener with everything needed for healthy plant growth almost completely automatically. Being able to have the peace of mind that you can never over water or over feed your plants again is one of the joys of hydroponic gardening.

Imagine how much time and money you could save by not having to go to the store for your tomatoes, herbs, lettuce, peppers and all the other fresh veggies you love to eat. How many times have you purchased fresh herbs and ended up throwing them away because they have wilted and lost their freshness? Hydroponic gardening allows you to pick as much or as little off the plant whenever you like. Fresh home grown tomatoes are so delicious that once you taste them I'm sure you will never buy another tomato in your life.

Plants grown traditionally in the soil are left to "fend for themselves" by having to get the nutrients they need to grow from the soil. Plants grown hydroponically are given food and water directly to the roots. This allows the hyrdroponically grown plants to grow faster and larger.

Another benefit to growing plants in hydroponic gardens is the space which is saved. The roots of plants grown in soil have to spread out far and wide to seek nutrients. The roots from plants in hydroponic gardens don't have to spread out so far. They are getting their nutrients directly on their roots. Therefore, they don't have to spread out so far. Therefore, you can have more plants in the same amount of space by using hydroponics.

Soil grown plants have to rely on the natural environment for such things as humidity, light, and temperature. The plants in hydroponic gardens can be given whatever amount of light, humidity, and temperature they need on a consistent basis, unlike their soil based counterparts.

Soil based plants are susceptible to pests, weeds, and soil borne diseases. With hydroponic gardens these concerns vanish. The pests that live in soil can not attack the plants. Also, because there is no soil, weeds cannot grow. The same goes for the soil borne diseases. No soil means the plants cannot get sick from common soil based diseases.

Growing soil based plants generally takes a lot of hard work. It takes a lot of commitment and a real "green thumb." Hydroponics, on the other hand, is a relatively simple way to grow plants. Very rarely could you neglect soil based plants for any length of time. They need to be tended to almost daily. This is not true with hydroponic gardens. The process can be fully automated. Another fantastic benefit is;

hydroponic gardens use way less water. Typically, the water in hydroponic gardens is recycled. Traditional farming wastes a large amount of water. The water is wasted through runoff and evaporation.

As you can see, the benefits to hydroponic gardening are numerous. The reasons to grow plants hydroponically largely outweigh those of traditional farming. Hydroponic gardening doesn't require you to have a "green thumb." Hydroponic gardening is easy, safe, and fun.

Due to the huge success of this unique and fun method of gardening, there are now over 100 hydroponic gardening centers in the United States and that figure is continuing to grow. Exactly what is so great about this type of gardening and what are its benefits?

1. No soils needed

In a sense, you can grow crops in places where the land is limited, doesn't exist, or is heavily contaminated. In the 1940s, Hydroponics was successfully used to supply fresh vegetables for troops in Wake Island, a refueling stop for Pan American airlines. This is a distant arable area in the Pacific Ocean. Also, Hydroponics has been considered as the farming of the future to grow foods for astronauts in the space (where there is no soil) by NASA.

2. Make better use of space and location

Because all that plants need are provided and maintained in a system, you can grow in your small apartment, or the spare bedrooms as long as you have some spaces. Plants' roots usually expand and spread out in search of foods, and oxygen in the soil. This is not the case in Hydroponics, where the roots are sunk in a tank full of oxygenated nutrient solution and directly contact with vital minerals. This means you can grow your plants much closer, and consequently huge space savings.

3. Climate control

Like in greenhouses, hydroponic growers can have total control over the climate - temperature, humidity, light intensification, the composition of the air. In this sense, you can grow foods all year round regardless of the season. Farmers can produce foods at the appropriate time to maximize their business profits.

4. Hydroponics is water-saving

Plants grown hydroponically can use only 10% of water compared to field-grown ones. In this method, water is recirculated. Plants will take up the necessary water, while run-off ones will be captured and return to the system. Water loss only occurs in two forms - evaporation and leaks from the system (but an efficient hydroponic setup will minimize or don't have any leaks).

It is estimated that agriculture uses up to 80% water of the ground and surface water in the US. While water will become a critical issue in the future when food production is predicted to increase by 70% according to the FAQ, Hydroponics is considered a viable solution to large-scale food production.

5. Effective use of nutrients

In Hydroponics, you have a 100% control of the nutrients (foods) that plants need. Before planting, growers can check what plants require and the specific amounts of nutrients needed at particular stages and mix them with water accordingly. Nutrients are conserved in the tank, so there are no losses or changes of nutrients like they are in the soil.

6. pH control of the solution

All of the minerals are contained in the water. That means you can measure and adjust the pH levels of your water mixture much more easily compared to the soils. That ensures the optimal nutrients uptake for plants.

7. Better growth rate

Is hydroponically plants grown faster than in soil? Yes, it is.

You are your own boss that commands the whole environment for your plants' growth - temperature, lights, moisture, and especially nutrients. Plants are placed in ideal conditions, while nutrients are provided at the sufficient amounts, and come into direct contacts with the root systems. Thereby, plants no longer waste valuable energy searching for diluted nutrients in the soil. Instead, they shift all of their focus on growing and producing fruits.

8. No weeds

If you have grown in the soil, you will understand how irritating weeds cause to your garden. It's one of the most time-consuming tasks for gardeners - till, plow, hoe, and so on. Weeds are mostly associated with the soil. So eliminate soils, and all bothers of weeds are gone.

9. Fewer pests & diseases

And like weeds, getting rids of soils helps make your plants less vulnerable to soil-borne pests like birds, gophers, groundhogs; and diseases like Fusarium, Pythium, and Rhizoctonia species.Also when growing indoors in a closed system, the gardeners can easily take controls of most surrounding variables.

10. Less use of insecticide, and herbicides

Since you are using no soils and while the weeds, pests, and plant diseases are heavily reduced, there are fewer chemicals used. This helps you grow cleaner and healthier foods. The cut of insecticide and herbicides is a strong point of Hydroponics when the criteria for modern life and food safety are more and more placed on top.

11. Labor and time savers

Besides spending fewer works on tilling, watering, cultivating, and fumigating weeds and pests, you enjoy much time saved because plants' growth is proven to be higher in Hydroponics. When agriculture is planned to be more technology-based, Hydroponics has a room in it.

12. Hydroponics is a stress-relieving hobby

This interest will put you back in touch with nature. Tired after a long working day and commute, you return to your small apartment corner, it's time to lay back everything and play with your hydroponic garden. Reasons like lack of spaces are no longer right. You can start fresh, tasty vegetables, or vital herbs in your small closets, and enjoy the relaxing time with your little green spaces.

Seem like there are lots of benefits of Hydroponics and the image below seems to try to persuade you into Hydroponic growing. But keep reading to learn about its downsides.

HYDROPONICS FUNDAMENTALS – PH, OXYGEN, NUTRIENT SOLUTIONS AND MORE

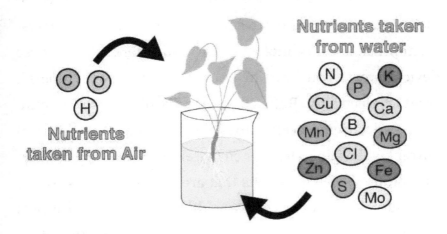

The more you know, the easier it is to grow!

CARBON DIOXIDE

During photosynthesis, plants use carbon dioxide (CO_2), light, and hydrogen (usually water) to produce carbohydrates, which is a source of food. Oxygen is given off in this process as a by-product. Light is a key variable in photosynthesis.

CONDUCTIVITY

Measuring nutrient solution strength is a relatively simple process. However, the electronic devices manufactured to achieve this task are quite sophisticated and use the latest microprocessor technology. To understand how these devices work, you have to know that pure water doesn't conduct electricity. But as salts are dissolved into the pure water, electricity begins to be conducted. An electrical current will begin to flow when live electrodes are placed into the solution. The more salts that are dissolved, the stronger the salt solution and, correspondingly, the more electrical current that will flow. This current flow is connected to special electronic circuitry that allows the grower to determine the resultant strength of the nutrient solution. The scale used to measure nutrient strength is electrical conductivity (EC) or conductivity factor (CF). The CF scale is most commonly used in hydroponics. It spans from 0 to more than 100 CF units. The part of the scale generally used by home hydroponic gardeners spans 0-100 CF units. The part of the scale generally used by commercial or large-scale hydroponic growers is from 2 to 4 CF. (strength for growing watercress and some fancy lettuce) to as high as approximately 35 CF for fruits, berries, and ornamental trees. Higher CF values are used by experienced commercial growers to obtain special plant responses and for many of the modern hybrid crops, such as tomatoes and some peppers. Most other plant types fall between these two figures and the majority is grown at 13-25 CF.

GERMINATION

When a seed first begins to grow, it is germinating. Seeds are germinated in a growing medium, such as perlite. Several factors are involved in this process. First, the seed must be active--and alive--and not in dormancy. Most seeds have a specific temperature range that must be achieved. Moisture and oxygen must be present. And, for some seeds, specified levels of light or darkness must be met. Check the specifications of seeds to see their germination requirements. The first two leaves that sprout from a seed are called the seed leaves, or cotyledons. These are not the true leaves of a plant. The seed develops these first leaves to serve as a starting food source for the young, developing plant.

GROWING MEDIUM

Soil is never used in hydroponic growing. Some systems have the ability to support the growing plants, allowing the bare roots to have maximum exposure to the nutrient solution. In other systems, the roots are supported by a growing medium. Some types of media also aid in moisture and nutrient retention. Different media are better suited to specific plants and systems. It is best to research all of your options and to get some recommendations for systems and media before making investing in or building an operation. Popular growing media include:

Composted bark. It is usually organic and can be used for seed germination.

Expanded clay. Pellets are baked in a very hot oven, which causes them to expand, creating a porous end product.

Gravel. Any type can be used. However, gravel can add minerals to nutrient. Always make sure it is clean.

Oasis. This artificial, foam-based material is commonly known from its use as an arrangement base in the floral industry.

Peat moss. This medium is carbonized and compressed vegetable matter that has been partially decomposed.

Perlite. Volcanic glass is mined from lava flows and heated in furnaces to a high temperature, causing the small amount of moisture inside to expand. This converts the hard glass into small, sponge-like kernels.

Pumice. This is a glassy material that is formed by volcanic activity. Pumice is lightweight due to its large number of cavities produced by the expulsion of water vapor at a high temperature as lava surfaces.

Rockwool. This is created by melting rock at a high temperature and then spinning it into fibers.

Sand. This medium varies in composition and is usually used in conjunction with another medium.

Vermiculite. Similar to perlite except that it has a relatively high cation exchange capacity-- meaning it can hold nutrients for later use.

There are a number of other materials that can (and are) used as growing media. Hydroponic gardeners tend to be an innovative and experimental group.

HYDROPONIC SYSTEMS

The apparatuses used in hydroponic growing are many and varied. There are two basic divisions between systems: media-based and water culture. Also, systems can be either active or passive. Active systems use pumps and usually timers and other electronic gadgets to run and monitor the operation. Passive systems may also incorporate any number of gadgets.

However, they to not use pumps and may rely on the use of a wicking agent to draw nutrient to the roots. Media-based systems--as their name implies--use some form of growing medium. Some popular mediabased systems include ebb-and-flow (also called flood-and-drain), run-to-waste, drip-feed (or top-feed), and bottom-feed. Water culture systems do not use media. Some popular water culture systems are raft (also called floating and raceway), nutrient film technique (NFT), and aeroponics.

LIGHT

Think of a plant as a well-run factory that takes delivery of raw materials and manufactures the most wondrous products. Just as a factory requires a reliable energy source to turn the wheels of its machinery, plants need an energy source in order to grow.

Artificial Light : Usually, natural sunlight is used for this important job. However, during the shorter and darker days of winter, many growers use artificial lights to increase the intensity of light (for photosynthesis) or to expand the daylight length. While the sun radiates the full spectrum (wavelength or color of light) suitable for plant life, different types of artificial lighting are selected for specific plant varieties and optimum plant growth characteristics. Different groups of plants respond in physically different ways to various wavelengths of radiation. Light plays an extremely important role in the production of plant material. The lack of light is the main inhibiting factor in plant growth. If you reduce the light by 10 percent, you also reduce crop performance by 10 percent. Light transmission should be your major consideration when purchasing a growing structure for a protected crop. Glass is still the preferred material for covering greenhouses because, unlike plastic films and sheeting, its light transmission ability is indefinitely maintained. No gardener can achieve good results without adequate light. If you intend to grow indoors, avail yourself of some of the reading material that has been published on this subject. If you are having trouble growing good plants, then light is the first factor to question.

Natural Light: A large part of the success in growing hydroponically is planning where to place the plants. Grow plants that have similar growing requirements in the same system. Placing your system 1-2 feet away from a sunny window will give the best results for most herbs and vegetables. Even your regular house lights help the plants to grow. Make sure that all of the lights are out in your growing area during the night. Plants need to rest a minimum of 4 hours every night. If your plants start to get leggy (too tall and not very full), move the system to a spot that has more sun. Once you find a good growing area, stick to it. Plants get used to their home location. It may take some time to get used to a new place.

MACRONUTRIENTS

Plants need around 16 mineral nutrients for optimal growth. However, not all these nutrients are equally important for the plant. Three major minerals--nitrogen (N), phosphorus (P), and potassium (K)--are used by plants in large amounts. These three minerals are usually displayed as hyphenated numbers, like "15-30-15," on commercial fertilizers. These numbers correspond to the relative percentage by weight of each of the major nutrients--known as macronutrients--N, P, and K. Macronutrients are present in large concentrations in plants. All nutrients combine in numerous ways to help produce healthy plants. Usually, sulfur (S), calcium (Ca), and magnesium (Mg) are also considered macronutrients.

These nutrients play many different roles in plants. Here are some of their dominant functions:

Nitrogen (N)--promotes development of new leaves

Phosphorus (P)--aids in root growth and blooming

Potassium (K)--important for disease resistance and aids growth in extreme temperatures

Sulfur (S)--contributes to healthy, dark green color in leaves

Calcium (Ca)--promotes new root and shoot growth

Magnesium (Mg)--chlorophyll, the pigment that gives plants their green color and absorbs sunlight to make food, contains a Mg ion

MICRONUTRIENTS

Boron (B), copper (Cu), cobalt (Co), iron (Fe) manganese (Mn), molybdenum (Mo), and zinc (Zn) are only present in minute quantities in plants and are known as micronutrients. Plants can usually acquire adequate amounts of these elements from the soil, so most commercial fertilizers don't contain all of the micronutrients. Hydroponic growers, however, don't have any soil to provide nutrients for their plants. Therefore, nutrient solution that is marketed for hydroponic gardening contain all the micronutrients.

NUTRIENT SOLUTION

In hydroponics, nutrient solution--sometimes just referred to as "nutrient"--is used to feed plants instead of plain water. This is due to the fact that the plants aren't grown in soil. Traditionally, plants acquire most of their nutrition from the soil. When growing hydroponically, you need to add all of the nutrients a plant needs to water. Distilled water works best for making nutrient. Hydroponic supply stores have a variety of nutrient mixes for specific crops and growth cycles. Always store solutions out of direct sunlight to prevent any algae growth. See also conductivity, macronutrients, and micronutrients.

Disposal Unlike regular water, you need to be careful where you dispose of nutrient. Even organic nutrients and fertilizers can cause serious imbalances in aquatic ecosystems. If you do not live near a stream, river, lake or other water source, it is fine to use old nutrient on outdoor plants and lawn. Another possibility is to use it on houseplants. However, if you live within 1,000 feet of a viable water source, do not use your spent nutrient in the ground.

OSMOSIS

The ends of a plant's roots aren't open-ended like a drinking straw and they definitely doesn't suck up a drink of water or nutrients. Science is still seeking a complete understanding of osmosis, so to attempt a full and satisfactory description of all that's involved in this process would be impossible. However, we can understand the basic osmotic principle as it relates to plants. First, consider a piece of ordinary blotting paper, such as the commonly used filter for home coffee machines. The paper might appear to be solid.

However, if you apply water to one side of it, you'll soon see signs of the water appearing on the opposite side. The walls of a feeding root act in much the same way. If you pour water onto the top of the filter paper, gravity allows the water to eventually drip through to the bottom side. Add the process of osmosis and water that's applied to the bottom side drips through to the top. With plants, this action allows water and nutrients to pass through the root walls from the top, sides, and bottom. Osmosis is the natural energy force that moves elemental ions through what appears to be solid material. A simplistic explanation for how osmosis works, although not 100 percent accurate, is that the stronger ion attracts the weaker through a semipermeable material.

So, the elements within the cells that make up plant roots attract water and nutrients through the root walls when these compounds are stronger than the water and nutrients applied to the outside of the roots. It then follows that if you apply a strong nutrient to the plant roots--one that's stronger than the compounds inside of the root--that the reverse action is likely to occur! This process is called reverse osmosis. Many gardeners have at some time committed the sin of killing their plants by applying too strong a fertilizer to their plants, which causes reverse osmosis. Instead of feeding the plant, they have actually been dragging the life force out of it.

Understanding how osmosis works, the successful grower can wisely use this knowledge to promote maximum uptake of nutrients into the plants without causing plant stress--or worse, plant death--from over fertilizing. All plants have a different osmotic requirement or an optimum nutrient strength.

OXYGEN

As a result of the process of photosynthesis, oxygen (O) is given off by plants. Then, at night, when light isn't available for photosynthesis, this process is reversed. At night, plants take in oxygen and consume the energy they have stored during the day.

PESTS AND DISEASES

Even though hydroponic gardeners dodge a large number of plant problems by eschewing soil (which is a home to any number of plant enemies), pests and diseases still manage to wreak havoc from time to time. Botrytis, Cladosporium, Fusarium, and Verticillium cover most of the genera of bacteria that can threaten your plants. The insects that can prove annoying include aphids, caterpillars, cutworms, fungus gnats, leaf miners, nematodes, spider mites, thrips, and whiteflies.

A few good ways to prevent infestation and infection are to:

Always maintain a sanitary growing environment

Grow naturally selected disease- and pest-resistant plant varieties

Keep your growing area properly ventilated and at the correct temperatures for your plants

Keep a close eye on your plants so if a problem does occur, you can act quickly

With insects, sometimes you can pick off and crush any large ones. Or you can try to wash the infected plants with water or a mild soap solution (such as Safer Soap). If a problem gets out of control, it may be necessary to apply a biological control in the form of a spray. Research which product will work best in your situation. Always follow the instructions on pesticides very closely. Alternatively, there are a number of control products on the market today that feature a botanical compound or an ingredient that has been synthesized from a plant material.

On botanical compounds as controlling agents: Over the last few years, researchers from all around the world have started to take a much closer look at any compounds present in the plant kingdom that might hold the answer to our pest and disease control problems. Many companies have even switched from producing synthetic pesticides to copying nature by synthesizing naturally occurring compounds in a laboratory setting. Extracts of willow, cinnamon, grapefruit, garlic, neem, bittersweet, lemon grass, derris, eucalyptus, and tomato have been helpful in controlling diseases and pests.

pH

The pH of a nutrient solution is a measurement of its relative concentration of positive hydrogen ions. Negative hydroxyl ions are produced by the way systems filter and mix air into the nutrient solution feeding plants. Plants feed by an exchange of ions. As ions are removed from the nutrient solution, pH rises. Therefore, the more ions that are taken up by the plants, the greater the growth. A solution with a pH value of 7.0 contains relatively equal concentrations of hydrogen ions and hydroxyl ions. When the pH is below 7.0, there are more hydrogen ions than hydroxyl ion. Such a solution "acidic." When the pH is above 7.0, there are fewer hydrogen ions than hydroxyl ions. This means that the solution is "alkaline."

Test the pH level of your nutrient with a kit consisting of vials and liquid reagents. These kits are available at local chemistry, hydroponic, nursery, garden supplier, or swimming pool supply stores. It is also a good idea to test the pH level of your water before adding any nutrients. If your solution is too alkaline add some acid. Although such conditions rarely occur, sometimes you may have to reduce the level of acidity by making the solution more alkaline. This can be achieved by adding potassium hydroxide (or potash) to the solution in small amounts until it is balanced once again.

PHOTOSYNTHESIS

Plants need to absorb many necessary nutrients from the nutrient solution or in the case of traditional agriculture, the soil. However, plants can create some of their own food. Plants use the process of photosynthesis to create food for energy. Carbohydrates are produced from carbon dioxide (CO_2) and a source of hydrogen (H) such as water in chlorophyll-containing plant cells when they are exposed to light. This process results in the production of oxygen (O).

PLANT PROBLEMS

Every now and again, you are sure to run into a problem with your plants. This is just a simple fact of any type of gardening. The key is to act quickly, armed with quality knowledge.

- *Mineral Deficiency Symptoms*

Nitrogen deficiency will cause yellowing of the leaves, especially in the older leaves. The growth of new roots and shoots is stunted. In tomatoes, the stems may take on a purple hue. A phosphorous deficiency is usually associated with dark green foliage and stunted growth. As in nitrogen deficiency, the stems may appear purple. But since the leaves don't yellow as they do in nitrogen deficiency, the whole plant can take on a purplish green color. Iron deficiency results in yellowing between the leaf veins. In contrast to nitrogen deficiency, the yellowing first appears in the younger leaves. After a prolonged absence of iron, the leaves can turn completely white.

- Wilting

This condition can be caused by environmental factors or disease (usually caused by Fusarium). Nutrient and media temperature can be adjusted to remedy wilt. However, if Fusarium have taken hold, the chances that your plants will survive are slim.

If wilting is due to environmental causes:

Try to spray the plants and roots with cool, clean water to rejuvenate them. If this hasn't helped them by the next day, try it again. If the plants respond, top-off the nutrient solution and check the pH. If the plants don't respond to the misting, empty the tank, move it to a shadier spot, and refill with cool, fresh nutrient solution. Don't reuse the old solution--start with fresh water and nutrients.

If wilting is due to a system blockage of nutrient:

For instance, tomato plants could be so dehydrated due to a nutrient supply blockage that they would be lying flat and for all the world looked stone-cold dead. When the nutrient flow resums and the plants are given the less stressful environment of nighttime, they tend to rebound so well that you'll be left wondering if they were the same plants few days ago.

PROPAGATION

Plants can be propagated by a number of methods. Growers can let a plant go to seed, collect the seeds, and then start the cycle over again (see germination). Another method is to take stem cuttings, which is also known as cloning (because you are creating an exact copy of the parent plant). Although this process won't work with all plants, it is a highly effective technique. Simply cut off a side shoot or the top of the main shoot just below a growth node. Make sure that there are at least two growth nodes above the cut. Remove any of the lower leaves near the base of the new plant. This cutting can then be rooted by placing it in water or in a propagation medium (perlite works well) that is kept moist. The use of some rooting hormone can help your chances of success.

PRUNING

Remove any discolored, insect-eaten, or otherwise sick-looking leaves from plants. Picking off some outer leaves or cutting the top off a plant can help it grow fuller. Use sharp scissors to prune your plants. Sometimes you will want to prune a plant to focus its energy on the remaining shoots. Pruning is an art and should be performed with care. Damaged or dying roots may also need to be pruned from time to time.

SOIL

Never use soil during any aspect of hydroponics. If you ever move a plant from a soil-based situation to hydroponics, remove all traces of soil or potting mix from the roots. Soil holds lots of microbes and other organisms and materials that love to grow in and contaminate your hydroponic system. Some of these will actually parasitize your plant and slow its growth. This is another advantage of hydroponic growing: The plant can get on with growing without having to support a myriad of other organisms as happens in conventional soil growing.

TEMPERATURE

Different plants have different germination and growing temperatures. Always make sure that you check each plant's growing requirements--especially minimum and maximum temperature levels. Keep in mind that specific varieties of plants may have different requirements.

WATER

Because the water supply is the source of life for your plants, quality is important. All plants rely on their ability to uptake water freely. Between 80 and 98 percent of this uptake is required for transpiration (loosely compared to perspiration in animals), which allows the plant to produce and somewhat control its immediate microclimate. Plants also need clean, uncontaminated water to produce their own healthy food supply.

The water you use in your hydroponic system needs to be pure. It is always a good idea to test your water source before adding nutrients so you aren't adding an element that is already present. In small systems, it would be wise to use distilled water. If you are starting a larger hydroponic operation, it would be a good idea to have a water analysis completed. Factors such as sodium chloride (NaCl, or salt) content and hardness will be of great use to growers. Also, groundwater can have elements normally not present in conditioned water. A key piece of advice: Get to know your water!

BUILD YOUR OWN HYDROPONICS SYSTEM

Maybe you have been interested in building your own

garden, but you are unsure about where to start. Growing plants on your own is a learning process that will continue for a long time. Chances are that you will never know everything there is to know about it, but you can still learn a lot and grow your own plants relatively easy if you are willing to learn how to do it properly. There are a wide range of plant growing techniques available, and some of these are easier to use than others. Hydroponics is way to grow plants using water, air, and a nutrient solution instead of soil.

One of the first steps to take on your way to building your own garden is to decide exactly what you want to grow. Some people like to grow plants for aesthetic purposes. These people usually grow flowers, shrubs, or tree varieties for the purpose of creating a visually appealing garden. Others prefer to grow plants that serve a functional purpose, such as providing fruits and vegetables to eat from the comfort of home. Once know exactly what type of plants you want to grow, you can move on to deciding on the logistics of your garden area.

Hydroponic gardens can be built indoors or outdoors. Either way, the space you will require will depend on the amount of plants you would like to grow in one setting. However you choose to build your garden, keep in mind that you will be needing additional space simply for your own freedom of movement. A garden that looks more like a jungle will be much harder to maintain than a well-organized garden area with plenty of additional space for you to move around in and get close to the plants you are growing.

After setting aside an area of your property to be used as a garden, the next step is to set up your hydroponics system. If you are a beginner to the world of hydroponic gardening, it would be a good idea to purchase your hydroponics system as opposed to building on your own. This will help you to get a better idea of how to successfully grow your own plants without the use of soil. Further along, as you become more familiar with growing plants with hydroponics, you can move on to integrating your own methods into the overall framework of your garden, but at first it is always better to have an established garden model to follow.

You can find a wealth of information about hydroponics and the various plant growing systems available online. There are also many different online garden stores available from which you can purchase almost all of the materials you will need to set up your own garden. Apart from the equipment you will be needing, you can also find nutrient solutions and fertilizers that will be essential to the long-term success of your hydroponic garden.

Using hydroponics systems will allow your plants to grow about 50% faster than they would in regular soil. Hydroponics also yields better harvests because nutrients are delivered directly to the plants. Using hydroponics is the best way to garden for city dwellers like us with no worries about soil and space - just the plants!

In building your own hydroponics system at home, you will need these basic materials. You will need a reservoir, pots - made of nets or mesh, a growing medium, nutrient solution, air stones, air lines or tubing and an air pump. You also need some Styrofoam, a sharp knife or box cutter, and a tape measure.

First thing to do is to choose a good reservoir. You can use a bucket, fish tank or a bin. Any container as long as it fits all your prospected number of pots for your plants. You will also need to paint the bin black; this is necessary only if your reservoir is transparent. Because if light is allowed in it, this promotes the growth of algae and other hazardous that is bad for your plants.

Next, draw a straight line down the side of the reservoir tank to serve as gauge in monitoring water or nutrient solution level. Then, measure your tank using the tape measure, get the dimensions, and begin to cut the Styrofoam into pieces that are one fourth of an inch smaller than the size of the reservoir and fit it inside. This will be your floater and should be on top of the nutrient solution and can adjust to water level changes.

Now, cut holes where you can place your pots. Place them evenly on top of the Styrofoam, making sure that there is enough room for each to get enough sunlight. Make another hole on any end for the air to pass through freely. Grab your air pump and connect the free end of the tubing to the air stone.

Set your system up by filling the reservoir with the nutrient solution. Run the tubing through the end hole of the Styrofoam and place it in the reservoir. Now, fill the pots with the growing medium and plant the seeds in. Put them on the floater. Turn on the pump and voila! You are finished.

© Copyright 2021 by William Brown   pag.

65

Actually, you can purchase hydroponics or grow kits at shops online and near you. Most kits have everything! They include gardening supplies and the basic materials like seeds, nutrients, growing medium and other supplements. Some may include pipes, pumps, growing trays, reservoirs and other components depending really on what particular hydroponics system you choose to install.

There are lots of benefits for growers who build their own systems. From cost savings to ease of use, these systems can offer several productive results to your grow room even if you are new to growing. Once you set off on this course it is unlikely that you will ever buy a pre-built system again.

Starting is always the hardest part. Henry Ford used to say that there is no job that can't be done as long as you break it down to smaller jobs, so don't be overwhelmed. Start with a simple drawing of what you intend to do and see if it makes sense.

A couple of considerations will be that you will not be able to receive tech support on your system.

There are tons of articles and support for system building around the web. The other consideration is that your plants overall health and productiveness in now on YOU and your new system so I might encourage you to test your system first with one plant before rolling it out across your whole grow.

The beauty of a custom built hydroponic system far exceeds to concerns however in that building your own system will provide you full control on what goes where and in what quantity. There is really no other way for a grower to customize his or her room to produce the maximum yield out of whatever floor plan. So rid yourself of doubts and get to work, there is a lot to be done.A feeling you'll never forget

Making your own hydroponic system takes a lot of hard work and most of all - precision. "What doesn't kill you makes you stronger" might be a good slogan, but your plants don't really enjoy facing hardships. Once you've completed the system, you will want to test it with a plant or two, and if that goes well, you can load your girls in and begin growing in your unique and personalized hydroponic system.

What does a hydroponic system need?

A reservoir - for holding and mixing a nutrient solution

Water Delivery - generally plumbing of some type coupled with a pump or gravity assisted to deliver the water where it is needed.

A Medium - Whether you are using Hydroton "clay pellets", Rockwool, or Soil. You are going to need a medium to place your plant into. Usually these mediums are contained in a net pot or cloth pot within your hydroponic system.

You can also add air stones, water chillers, and a plethora of other features to govern water temperatures, oxygen density, and flow rate. But above are pretty much the essentials.

Caring for the plants is one thing. Getting the best out of them is another.

There are so many options out there for hydroponic systems. Recently a lot of growers have been going with personalized systems and there a hundreds of different offerings available all over the net. One great way to ensure your plants success is using the "pH perfect" line from Advanced Nutrients. This takes all of the headache out of continually having to pH your water.

Did you know that by maintaining perfect pH levels it can result in up to 30% greater yield? In the past this was very hard to do but with this new innovation in hydroponic nutrients, the scientists at Advanced Nutrients have done all of the work for you.

It is adivasable for you to not try to reinvent the wheel here. There are so many systems available that you should easily be able to find something that you like and that makes sense to you. Just try not to get carried away until you have built a couple and understand the general principals of the way water moves or you could very easily harm your plants and even flood, and floods really sucks.

Building a system is fun and generally less expensive than buying one. Just remember that everything needs to be clean so avoid using old hoses or a dirty old trashcan as a reservoir or it could stop you before you even get started in your new system. There are so many ways to go on this that the world is literally your oyster when it comes to hydroponic system building.

Irrigation, watering, stable net the plant can use to climb/grow upon and nutrient containers/reservoir. That's the basics. With some nutrients, you don't even need to check the pH levels of your plant's environment every hour or so - just let them do your magic. Hence, you don't need a pH meter for the system either.

Hydroponic indoor gardening systems, why would anyone want to garden indoors?

Have you ever wanted to turn off the rain? - Or maybe turn it on? How about the hot sun and temperatures of summer - would you like to be able to control that, too? And the pests! They seem ever abundant and know exactly where you have planted your prize vegetable.

Control ,yes, that is the reason so many gardeners are turning to hydroponic gardening - they can control the growing environment for their plants.

HYDROPONIC BASICS

Instead of using the soil, hydroponic indoor gardening requires only a growing medium and a nutrient solution - and lighting, of course. The roots of the plant are fed directly so they do not have to expend their energy "searching" for nutrients and water. This allows the plant to grow more quickly and with greater abundance. Hydroponic kits are available as well as much information for building your own hydroponic system.

CONCEPTS OF HYDROPONIC GARDENING - NUTRIENTS

Plants need several primary types of nutrients in order to grow. The three main elements needed are:

1. Nitrogen

2. Phosphorus

3. Potassium

Plants with these three nutrients in the proper balance will be enabled to grow their best.

Secondary elements needed for plants to grow healthy and strong are:

1. Calcium

2. Iron

3. Magnesium

4. Manganese

5. Zinc

6. Sodium

A proper balance of both the primary and secondary elements needed for plant growth will result in healthy, vegetable bearing plants.

The balance of these nutrients is important and needs to be monitored. Equipment is available to make this an easy step in your daily gardening activities.

CONCEPTS OF HYDROPONIC GARDENING - LIGHTING

Just as outdoor plants benefit from the light of the sun, indoor plants benefit from a good lighting system. Different types of lighting can be used. Each has different effects on the plants that are grown.

Plants use different types of light during the different cycle of their growth. Plants will use blue light when they are on a high growth cycle, and a red or orange light of the color spectrum when they are in the flowering stage. Lighting systems to meet the needs of your growing plants are easily installed in your hydroponic garden.

HOW TO MAINTAIN A HYDROPONIC SYSTEM

Unlike plants in soil, the roots of hydroponic plants are provided with water, oxygen and nutrients through one of several hydroponics systems. The big challenge is to make certain the nutrient solution is keeping up with your plant needs. At the same time, it's necessary to avoid excesses or deficiencies of minerals, extremes in pH, temperature or a lack of oxygen.

DON'T TAKE YOUR WATER FOR GRANTED

Because your nutrient solution is made up mostly of water, the quality of your water is important. If you're using well water or water from any other source, you have to check it regularly with a dissolved solids meter (PPM).

After testing, you may find your water contains high levels of salts like Calcium and Magnesium carbonates these are among the most common minerals found in excessive amounts.

Generally, a calcium content of more than 200 PPM or 75 PPM of magnesium can be on the edge of excessive. This can create a situation called 'lock-out'. When lock-out occurs, other important elements or minerals can become unavailable to your plants.

If you find your water is hard or contaminated with excessive amounts of any element, your best recourse may be a water purification system. One of the best is a system called 'RO (reverse osmosis'.

WATCH THAT TEMPERATURE

Your plants generally will appreciate root zone temperatures between 65 degrees (18 C) and 80 degrees (27 C). The solution can be a little cooler for winter crops and a little warmer for tropical plants.

If your solution is too cold, seeds won't germinate, cuttings won't root and plants will tend to grow more slowly. In some instances your plants will stop growing altogether and die. The same applies if you allow the root mass to become too hot.

Also keep in mind that plants don't like rapid changes in temperatures, particularly in the root zone. So, when adding water to your reservoir, the best practice is to let it sit long enough to reach the same temperature as the water in the reservoir.

KEEPING WATCH OVER THE PH

The best way to control pH is to mix fresh hydroponic nutrients with your water and let it stand to stabilize the pH. After it is stabilized, you can add products to increase or lower the pH.

Most plants prefer a pH that's between 5.8 and 6.3. Keep in mind that it's common for pH to drift up for a while, then down, then back up again. You can safely allow this drift to range between 5.5 and 7.0 without adjusting it. In fact, it's better for your plants if you don't keep dumping a lot of chemicals into your solution to try and maintain a perfect 5.8 to 6.3.

WHEN TO CHANGE YOUR NUTRIENT SOLUTION

When you start out with a fresh solution in your reservoir, note the date, pH and EC or PPM.

When the reservoir level drops, note the EC/PPM level and top it off with fresh water.

Retest the EC/PPM. If the nutrient strength has dropped significantly, add a bit more nutrient.

Always record how much water you add to top-off your reservoir. When the total amount of water you've added equals the capacity of your reservoir, it's time to drain and replace all of your nutrient solution.

BEWARE OF DISEASE IN YOUR SOLUTION

Perhaps one of the most important things you can do to keep your grow room disease free is keep it clean. Be particularly careful about allowing soil to be accidentally kicked or dropped into your solution. If this happens, all your hard work could end up for nothing.

If you see evidence of disease in any single plant, get rid of it immediately. Then keep a close watch on your other plants and destroy any that show the same symptoms. Then completely drain and renew your nutrient solution. If possible, flush your entire system by running fresh water through it without any nutrients. It's better to lose a few plants than your entire harvest.

POTENTIAL PROBLEMS AND HOW TO OVERCOME THEM

From time to time, hydroponic growers may face problems with their hydroponic systems and plants. Some problems can easily be resolved without causing too much stress. But there are some issues that can be quite confusing even for the most experienced grower. The most common issues in hydroponic gardens usually involve nutrient deficiency, algae growth, pests and pathogens. If you're new to this type of gardening, being aware of the common problems that you may encounter and the best ways to fix them is important in order to produce healthy and high yielding plants.

NUTRITION DEFICIENCY

The correct composition and formulation of your nutrient solution is essential to provide your plants with all the required nutrients for optimal growth and higher yields. However, the composition of nutrient solution changes as they flow throughout the root system and mineral ions are extracted.

The most common nutrient deficiency problems in various plant species are potassium, nitrogen, magnesium, iron and calcium. Iron deficiency is quite common under cool growing environment, where the root system is saturated or severely damaged or where there are high levels of ph. Magnesium deficiency on the other hand, is often caused by high levels of potassium in the solution. Calcium deficiency is usually the result of high humidity which hampers transpiration and proper distribution of calcium.

Generally, the key to avoiding nutrient deficiency problems in plants is to keep accurate measurements. Being able to get accurate measurements of the solution's conductivity, temperature, pH level and other important elements of the system allows you to react to various conditions before they create nutrient deficiency problems.

ALGAE GROWTH

Typically, the water, nutrients and light in your system induces algae growth. It usually appears as a green, reddish, black or brown, slimy growth that clings to gullies, channels and pumps or develops on the surface of your growth media. Algae produce a moldy or earthy smell. In addition to the unsightly appearance and unpleasant odor of algae, they can also block the dripper, pumps, emitter, filters and return channels of your system. Heavy growth can also spread over the growing substrates and the roots of oxygen.

Some growers tolerate little amounts of algae growth in the system as long as it does not grow thick and widespread. A small growth doesn't usually cause any problem. But when the growth has become excessive, your best option is to get the whole system cleaned up after crop removal and then start all over again with a clean and algae-free system.

PESTS AND PATHOGENS

Most indoor hydroponic gardens get attacked by various pests and pathogens such as spider mites, fungus gnats, white flies, pythium and aphids. Diseases such as fungi or mold may also affect the healthy growth of your plants. In order to produce healthy crop, growers have several treatment methods to choose from such as commercial pesticide, biological control or specially formulated products for eliminating hydroponic garden pests.

TIPS AND TRICKS FOR BUILDING YOUR OWN HYDROPONIC GARDEN

In today's society, more and more people are taking up hydroponics gardening as a hobby. If you want to build a hydroponic garden, there are many plans and designs available. This type of gardening does not require the amount of space that backyard gardening does.

The First Steps-the Aggregate System: The first step to build a hydroponic garden is to decide the kind of hydroponic system that you want to use. For beginners, the aggregate system is the easiest system to build and maintain. Aggregate are substances such as gravel or sand that you can place your plants in to give them extra support. This type of system consists of a plant tank and a nutrient tank, with hoses that run between the two. The plants are fed by opening the nutrient tank so that it floods the plant tank. Then the solution is drained immediately, leaving valuable nutrients and water clinging to the plant roots that will keep them fed until the next flooding. The draining process serves to aerate the solution so that outside aerating sources such as air pumps are not necessary.

If you decide to build a hydroponic system using an aggregate system, you will first need to build a container. Your container measurements will be determined by the amount of space that you have available as well as the type of plants that you wish to grow. Low-lying plants will need less space than plants that grow on vines. So you need to adjust the height of your container accordingly.

You also need to have a separate nutrient container, which can be a fifty gallon drum for larger areas or five gallon buckets for smaller ones. You will need to hook up hoses and an air compressor system that will allow you to run the nutrients from the source container to the plant tank.

This type of hydroponic system will also need a lighting device. For specific instructions, as to how to build a hydroponic garden using the aggregate system, you can contact your local gardening store.

The First Steps-the Water Culture Hydroponic System Simply put, the water culture system is defined as a system where the plants are put directly in a nutrient solution. The first step to build a hydroponic garden using a water culture system is to construct a container that is waterproof. You need to make sure that the container will not leak out the nutrients that are vital to keeping your plans healthy. You will also need to have a built-in drainage system as the nutrient solution will need to be drained every week for younger plants and every two weeks for more mature plants.

To build a hydroponic garden using this system, you will also need to install an air pump system. The nutrient solution needs to be continually aerated, so you will need an air pump that runs nonstop. Depending on the maturity of the plants in the container, a gently running air pump system may be your best bet.

The First Steps-the Aeroponics System
If you want to build a hydroponics garden, the aeroponics hydroponics system is the most advanced and the most difficult to build. You will need to build a container that will allow no light to reach your plants. You will also need to build in spray nozzles that will continually spray your plants with a mist of nutrient solution. The humidity level inside your container should be almost 100% at all times. Due to the amount of nutrient solution that you will need to use, you will probably want to use a fifty five gallon drum. A low-powered

air compressor will also need to be used with this type of hydroponics system.

The Expense

If you are interested in how to build a hydroponic garden, be advised. The materials needed for this type of gardening can be very expensive. For more information, you can contact your garden supply center.

A hydroponic system is a very complex setup, and there is much information which needs to be learned about it. The process of understanding how to make a hydroponic system is one in which there are lots of steps involved, so the person creating it has to become really patient. That is however only the case if you want to build a system from scratch, you can also buy system like a HydroHut Deluxe and then all the figuring out has been done for you.

STEP BY STEP

One of the very first and most essential points anyone understanding how to make a hydroponic system needs to learn is that the actual layout of the system is actually only going to be restricted by the desires of the designer. In other words, you can truly go full-scale and build whichever sort of hydroponic structure that you want.

An additional step in understanding how to make a hydroponic system is to gather the required components. These will certainly vary according to what the creator wants the system to look like, but one of the most standard and essential items is a ordinary tray. Remember that the system should provide means both to support the plant and to aerate the system. A person is able to create a more complex system with much more pricey materials but then at the same time they can also buy it for almost the same price.

An essential tip to remember when understanding how to make a hydroponic system, is that short plants for example lettuce and spinach will probably be able to support themselves and so these are truly the best options to go with since they will have less threat of suffering from complications. Additionally take into account that you will find some great hydroponic grow tents offered that one can purchase and which will probably be of great help.

You will find also a lot of great resources available that is going to be useful to any person trying to learn how to make a hydroponic system, in particular those on the Internet. This is since with the web an individual is able to browse through literally hundreds of diverse websites in a matter of minutes, something that obviously could not be done otherwise. The finest thing to do here would be to go on a search engine on the World wide web and type in "hydroponic grow tent" and then the diverse available options will pop up. Probably the most essential thing to bear in mind is that most simple and effective system is a HydroHut.

Learning how to make a hydroponic system is great. You are building a very powerful system that is able to grow plants better and faster than any other method we know of.

This is a simple system but can very effective. It works by using a fabric wick to soak up water and nutrients from a reservoir below. It is so good that you can leave it unattended for a few days at a time with no issues.

Below are the steps to show you how to make a hydroponic system;

For this system, use two containers, One larger (the water reservoir) and one smaller one (the container which holds the plant). The idea is to have the smaller container wedged into the larger container without touching the bottom of the larger container.

What sort of larger container should you use?

Use a bucket which has straight sides. Paint it black on the inside, to prevent algae from growing.

pag.

What sort of smaller container should you use?

Use a normal plastic plant pot, that is tapered (i.e. make sure that it is wider at the top than the bottom). Most plant pots fit this description. Ensure that the top of this container is wider than the top of the larger container.

Also make sure, that the bottom of the smaller container, is narrower than the top of the larger container. This container should slide inside the larger container, but not all the way. It should also not touch the bottom of the large container.

What do you do next?

Drill a hole in the bottom of the smaller container. Through this, thread a large cotton wick. You can use some thick cord from the hardware. Use a cord which is about half an inch thick.

Make sure it is long enough, to go from the water reservoir at the bottom, to halfway into the smaller container. The smaller container is where the plant and growing medium will be. The wick will constantly carry water and nutrients to the plant.

Also drill a hole in the side of the larger container just below where the small container sits. This will allow for any excess liquid, to drain out of the side of the larger container, and not flood the smaller container.

Fill the smaller container with a combination of Perlite and Vermiculite, ensuring that the wick goes well into the mixture. Your hydroponic system is now set up and ready for planting. Carefully wash any soil from the roots of the plant which you are going to use. Carefully plant it into its new home.

Now all you need to do is water your new plant with an appropriate nutrient solution. Make sure you water it enough, so that the water reservoir at the bottom fills up. All you need to do now is to check that the reservoir at the bottom does not run completely dry.

Whenever it is nearly empty, water it again to fill it up. In hot weather, this may be every few days, and in cool weather it may be every couple of weeks. That's all there is to setting up a hydroponic wick system.

Do you want to learn even more about hydroponics?

Hydroponics is constantly evolving. The more knowledge you have the more successful you will be. To really get great advice, on how to make a hydroponic system, read and watch hydroponic secrets. This is a key guide which will make you very successful, very quickly.

HOW TO PLANT, GERMINATE, TRANSPLANT, AND GROW SEEDLINGS

BASIC PRINCIPALS: Plant foliage requires light, oxygen and carbon dioxide. Plant root systems require water, nutrients and oxygen. When plants are grown normally water leeches nutrients from the soil and carries them to the roots. The water and nutrients are taken up by the roots to feed plant growth. Soil drainage then allows water to be replaced by air in the gaps between soil grains. This supplies the roots with oxygen. In hydroponics the nutrients are dissolved in the water.

Soil is replaced with a growing medium to supply the roots with water, nutrients and oxygen. Hydro juice (nutrient solution) can be drip fed to each plant, it can also be used to regularly flood the root chamber, then drain out. Both methods require a pump and timer to circulate the nutrients through the roots and are covered by these diagrams and notes. Roots can also be grown in the air by spraying roots with a fine mist of hydro juice, or grown in the hydro juice and the solution aerated under each root mass with an air pump. With both of the second two methods the plants must secured at the base of the stem or something.

The hydroponic system described does work and is suitable for any plant with stringy roots. I have not tried it with any bulb plants or plants such as orchids that require fungus or mold in the soil to grow. This method is similar to Nutrient Film Technique (NFT) the thin Rockwool slice acting as a capillary mat. This eliminates the need to have flat bottom the root chamber and to level the bottom of root chamber, making easier and cheaper to set up. This method will get the most vigorous growth if each plant has it's own continuos drip feed.

The dripper is positioned drip on roots growing from the base of the seedling block, the roots will grow thick, hairy and compact under the dripper. 4L per hour dripper are used however their drip rate depends pressure, this is effected by height and size of the drip feed tank. The drip rate will slow as the tank empties. Feeding can also be achieved with faster dripper at the top of each top end of each side of the root chamber. The plants grown like this had a large root mass, the roots of three plant taking up about a third of the root chamber. With the timer I had could only flood the root chamber every 4 hours, the growth rate was similar to the last. The growth rate will improve by flooding every hour or even less. After the root chamber is flooded it should drain to a trickle in a few minutes.

STARTING PLANTS: Soak seeds in damp paper or cotton wool, cover seed with damp paper or cloth, drian off excess water and don't allow to dry out. When the seed root is 2 - 5mm. long place the seed root first in the small hole with tweezers. Make sure the root is protected by the open jaws of the tweezers and that the seed or root isn't squashed. Then place seedling block hole up on a plate and wet Rockwool until it won't take any more water. Keep the plate on an angle for drainage, but the seedling blocks shouldn't dry out too much and seedling should come up in a few days. Seedlings can stay on the plate until roots grow from the bottom or sides of the seedling block.When this happens seedling are ready to transplanted on to the Rockwool mat in the root chamber. (Before the seedling blocks go into the root chamber the rookwool is soaked in water 24 hours then with hydro juice at half strength.)

Roots will grow from seedling block, through and along the under side of the Rockwool mats. Place three to eight plants per side, evenly spaced along the slot, and it will soon grow into mass of green. When the system is operational and plants are growing, the inside of the root chamber should have a rich earthy smell. Three or four plants if your growing them big (outdoors), eight if your growing fast and flowering early (under lights).

When the roots grow from the bottom or sides of the Rockwool block it's ready to transplant into the grow tube. Once the roots have grown into the mat tou can hit them with full stength hydro juice. Light proof plastic should be used to cover the top of the root chamber white side up, this is to stop green slime growing on the rockwool. This can only be done when the plant is tall enough, take care not strain or damage the plant.

Many seeds require special conditions to germinate. For example, most garden vegetables and herb seeds need to remain damp or wet for some time. Seeds can be germinated in a hydroponic grower, and often they germinate even better than in soil.

Planting Seeds

Most seeds are placed below the surface of the media. A suggested placement is from ½ to 1 inch below the surface. This keeps the seed very moist and will give it some feel for when the light is and where the dark is. The root of the plant will grow down towards the dark and the water, and the plant stem and leaves will go towards the light.

Many seed packets include instructions for soil and mention how deep to bury the seeds. They can be planted at the same depth in hydroponics. Some seeds, like beans and corn, will germinate in just a few days. Some others, such as tomato, bell pepper and herbs may take as long as two weeks until they appear. Growers with seeds should be watered each day although no plants are showing. If you do not see any sign of life after two weeks, it is best to replant the grower. Occasionally the grower root area will be so cold or so dry, the seeds will not germinate. To germinate very small seeds like many herbs, a special form of germination may be required. One way is to start the seeds between two pieces of paper or a towel soaked with water. The towel is kept moist each day. Germinating some types of seeds is more complicated than just soaking in water. Some seeds need to be damaged in some way to germinate, and others are specialized to respond to periods of temperature or light. If there something you would like to grow, it might help to learn what the seed requirements are to germinate.

Other Methods of Reproducing

Some plants can reproduce from cuttings. This means cutting a small part of the growing tip of a plant, pulling off the bottom leaves and sticking the cut end into the growing media. Some of the plants that can be reproduced from cuttings are basils and many of the herbs.

Garlic reproduces from individual garlic cloves. Some of the garlic in the grocery store is treated and will not sprout. An organic garlic is more likely to sprout.

Potatoes are grown from a planted potato. The potato can be cut into pieces or planted whole.

TROUBLESHOOTING COMMON PROBLEMS

If you've just set up or are now running a hydroponics garden, you will eventually have a problem and need to do some trouble shooting hydroponics system work. Usually, though, it's not as large a problem as it might seem. If you're using a pre-made kit, though, it can seem difficult since you didn't built it yourself, so you might not be as familiar with the parts as you would otherwise be.

That is still not a big deal, though. All hydroponics systems work in the same basic way and nearly all of their components are the same, when you boil it down. When you realize that fact and learn what those systems are and how they function, trouble shooting and fixing aren't a real worry.

With all of that in mind, let's go through the basics of a hydroponics system and then look at some common problems and solutions for one that's malfunctioning.

First, a typical hydroponics garden will consist of five basic parts: the trays (or "beds"), a circulation system for the nutrient solution, a grow light (or lights), and a suspension system or medium for the plants' support. The fifth part is the plants themselves, of course.

Common problems with hydroponic gardens usually revolve around the nutrient solution or the circulation system. So in most cases, trouble shooting hydroponics system problems center around these two elements.

Plants Sickly or Withering

If your plants are becoming sickly, beginning to wither, or aren't doing well otherwise, then your problem is likely in one of two places: the nutrient solution and its circulation or the light being provided.

Obviously, if it's the latter, you'll need to either increase, decrease, or move the lighting. "Burned" or "singed" plants mean the light is too close (it should be at least six to eight inches away from the leaves, according to the light manufacturer's recommendations).

Otherwise, your problems are in the nutrient solution. Make sure that it's circulating properly. See that it's going into the medium (or solution tray) and moving through to the drain without obstruction. Sometimes, the media will "clump" or have plant parts or other blockades disturbing the flow of nutrient solution. If you're using expanded clay or coir, be sure it's not clogged with leftover roots from previous plantings-a common problem with these mediums.

The solution itself should be checked for pH level using a testing dipper or simple test strips. Sometimes, especially as the plants go through their fastest growth periods (shortly before maturity), they will give off more wastes than otherwise. This can mean the solution is over-saturated with wastes, leading to higher acidity levels. This is remedied with a simple dilution of water or replacement of the nutrient solution altogether (best).

Nutrient Solution Not Circulating

The answer to this problem is likely the obvious one: is the pump working? Otherwise, the above checks for clear flow will probably find the problem.

Algae or Parasite Infestation

This is also a common problem, especially for deep water cultures. Algae often begins to grow on the sides of tanks or in the hoses connecting the solution circulation reservoir, pump, etc. The easy fix for most algae problems is to restrict its access to sunlight. Tanks, trays, and so forth should be dark (store-purchased kits are often deep green or black) to block sunlight infiltration. If they aren't, black garbage backs can be used to line them inside or out to block the light and do the job.

Parasites are another problem that can happen when the sterility of the system is compromised. Outdoor/greenhouse systems often have a problem with this. The usual parasite killers for gardening will work, either chemical or physical. A natural or organic method like diatomaceous earth or vinegar solution is most recommended, of course.

General Maintenance to Prevent Problems

Many problems with hydroponic systems come from older equipment failing and from improper maintenance. Be sure to maintain your system to keep this from happening. It's not very difficult, especially if you make a habit of it. The most often ignored duty is thorough cleaning of the entire setup between crops.

When the beds are empty and the solution has been dumped, use a thorough cleaning method to flush our the tubes, trays, medium, etc. Believe it or not, this flushing is similar to the way you clean out a drip coffee maker. A 1:5 vinegar-water solution run through a couple of times will do the job. Easy!

Most of the time, trouble shooting hydroponics system problems is fairly simple since hydroponics isn't nearly as complex as people who've never done it before might think.

CONCLUSION

In recent years hydroponics is seen as a promising strategy for growing different crops. As it is possible to grow short duration crop like vegetables round the year in very limited spaces with low labour, so hydroponics can play a great contribution in areas with limitation of soil and water and for the poorer and landless people. In India, the hydroponic industry is expected to grow exponentially in near future. To encourage commercial hydroponic farm, it is important to develop low cost hydroponic technologies that reduce dependence on human labour and lower overall startup and operational costs.

Hydroponics is a system used to grow plants in controlled conditions. The difference between hydroponic systems and traditional plant growing methods is that hydroponics relies on growing plants without soil. Instead, plants are grown in a water-based solution that is enriched with all of the nutrients and minerals that are essential to healthy plant growth. It is possible to grow almost any kind of plant or crop with a hydroponic system. The word hydroponics is basically a combination between the Greek word "hydro", meaning water, and "ponic", meaning labor.

Scientists first figured out the basics of hydroponics in the 19th century, when a team of specialized researchers discovered that plants do not require soil to absorb nutrients. Soil essentially works as a sort of growth pool where important nutrients and minerals are contained, but plants cannot actually absorb these nutrients until after water has been added. By removing soil and creating a water-based solution full of all the minerals and nutrients required by the plant in question, it is possible to grow virtually any plant successfully.

Many countries throughout the world have begun to use hydroponic systems to grow crops. There are numerous advantages to this modern type of plant cultivation. Notable advantages include an overall higher crop yield and more stable growth throughout the cultivation period. It is also notable more cost-effective to use hydroponics as a method of cultivation within the agricultural industry, because less nutrients are required to promote optimal plant growth than with regular soil. The reason for this is that plants require a variety of nutrients that are rarely found in a perfect balance within soil. When using a water-based system, however, it is possible to control exactly which nutrients are placed within the solution and in their exact quantities. This lowers the cost of soil enrichment and also helps to promote an environment where plants can thrive and produce high yield fruits, vegetables, and other crops. Also, because the controlled environment necessary for water-based plant growth, nutrition pollution is considerably minimized. The primary disadvantage of this type of system is that the high humidity levels and use of fertilizer can create a possible breeding environment for salmonella.

Hydroponic-based systems are becoming increasingly popular among agriculturalists and home garden owners alike. If you are interested in switching over to this cultivation system, there are many ways to do so. You will find that setting up a hydroponic is much easier when designed within an outdoor setting, as there are numerous challenges associated with creating a successful indoor hydroponic garden. However, with the right tools and circumstances it is possible to set your indoor garden up as well.

In conclusion, if you are interested in creating your own garden from scratch, consider using a hydroponic system to help you do this as easily as possible. There are a wide range of products that you can find from online retailers as well as detailed guides and accurate information on how to install and set up your very own hydroponic garden. Happy growing!

Whether your interest lies in growing flowers or vegetables, the Hydroponic Gardening System, is for you. It is an easy to start, low cost and highly productive and personally, a very rewarding recreation or past time, that will show maximum yield, flavour and colours to whatever you grow. Whether you garden for fun, food or for profit, you also get to reap the rewards of hydroponic gardening without breaking the bank.

Whether you have a big garden, a small one or live in a flat with just a couple of window boxes, this can be the start of a very enjoyable hobby for you.

A Brief History of Hydroponics

Hydroponics comes from two Greek words, "hydro" meaning water and "ponics" meaning labour, the concept of which has been around for thousands of years. Two early working examples of such a system are the Hanging Gardens of Babylon and The Floating Gardens of China.

So What Is Hydroponics?

Hydroponics is the art and practice of growing plants and vegetables in either a bath or flow of highly oxygenated, nutrient enriched water without having to use soil.

Imagine the ease and simplicity of growing a vegetable garden without having to worry about the soil or too little water or when to fertilize. And it works for both the beginner and the advanced grower! Hydroponic grown vegetables are healthy, vigorous and consistently reliable. Your flowers are bigger, stronger and more colourful and your gardening efforts are clean and tidy and extremely easy requiring very little effort on your part. Green fingers are definitely not required.

Are there Benefits to Using Hydroponics?

Well, the growth rate on a hydroponic plant is considered to be between 30-50 percent faster than a soil grown plant. The extra oxygen in the hydroponic growing medium helps to stimulate root growth. The nutrients in a hydroponic system are mixed with the water and sent directly to the root system where these nutrients are being delivered to the medium several times each day. The hydroponic plant requires very little energy to find and break down these food nutrients. The plant then uses this saved energy to help it grow faster and to produce more bloom or fruit, which in turn gives a much greater yield. In general, plants grown hydroponically are healthier and happier plants, which has to be a good thing I'm sure you would agree.

Hydroponic Systems

There are two types of Hydroponic systems, which are either active or passive. An active system moves the nutrient solution through a pump to feed the plant or vegetable. A passive system relies on the growth or capillary action of the growing medium being used. The nutrient solution is absorbed by the medium and passed along to the roots.

Should you Buy or Build a System yourself

Should I buy one or build one? Both have their merits. Obtaining an inexpensive system will allow you to get your feet wet, which will give you a hands on approach to understanding just how hydroponics works. Whereas, if you are mechanically minded, then building one will give you greater satisfaction but will take longer to set up. The end result of course will be the same.

The future of vegetable and flower growing is through the use of a Hydroponic Gardening System. It is fast becoming a very popular hobby. Above all else, it is fun, exciting and easy for people of any age, to get involved in.

CPSIA information can be obtained
at www.ICGtesting.com
Printed in the USA
LVHW022017220121
677171LV00007B/439